MEN

NEED

SPACE

D0839351

In the night bound world, I looked up.
Polaris was over head, and Arcturus.

I heard the Rabbi say,

The first marriage is of the body.
The second is the wine of love.
In the third, we marry with our eyes, only.
And in the fourth, only with our breath.

This book is dedicated to the Fourth Marriage.

MEN

NEED

SPACE

judyth hill

Blessings
Gratitude.

"Women Need Time! Forgiveness as much as men in Love who grant theirs"

SHERMAN
SASHER
Publishing

Acknowledgments

The following poems have previously appeared in: *The Goddess Cafe*, Fish Drum, Santa Fe, NM,1990: "10,000 Waves in Shoji Tub". *Hardwired for Love*, Pennywhistle Press, Santa Fe, NM,1991: "There is No Way to Love Without Being Changed," and "The Real Revolution (is Evolution)". "Paula's Story" first appeared in *The Denny Poems*, 1982 and won a Billee Murray Denny Poetry Award from the Illinios Arts Council, Spoonriver Press, Peoria, IL. *Baker's Baedeker*, Shacharit Press, Santa Fe, NM,1988: "Marriage is Not a Pretty Subject", "Weddings and Armed Robbery", and "Illinios Central". *Saludos: Poems of New Mexico*, Pennywhistle Press, Santa Fe, NM,1995: "Your Writing's Not in Cochiti".

First Edition
ISBN 0-9644196-3-7
Second Printing, 2000

Printed in the USA on acid free, recycled paper
Type set in Weiss® Adobe
Book design by Judith Rafaela
Cover Design by New Grub Street Design, Santa Fe, NM

Sherman Asher Publishing
PO Box 2853
Santa Fe, NM, 87504

Editor's Note

Judyth Hill is a performance poet who is described in reviews as "energy with skin." This collection, her sixth, brings together often performed and requested pieces on marriage, divorce, love, and passion. Arranged in tribute to growth, one moves from expectations to disillusion and disintegration, the passions of writing, to seeing people as they actually are, and love in its deepest sense. This book is sure to delight anyone in relationship.

Her poems move with the rhythm of breath and create challenges for setting into type words which ring with sound and motion. Yet those who only listen to the wild muse may miss the enormous scholarship, her apprenticeship to works of literature and art. She never stops teaching us about the craft of poetry. Her seminars are noted for her generosity as she brings others of all ages to appreciate poetry.

Special acknowledgment and thanks to Nancy Fay for her tireless work editing, arranging and rearranging the material. And what a joy it is to work with Judyth who tolerates endless fine tuning of punctuation, questioned word choices and points of grammar, and demands for shorter or longer pieces, as we commit to print the invocation of her cantor voice and the sounds of wild geese in flight.

Judith Rafaela

Table of Contents

It's an honor
to share what marries us,
late night romance to diapers,
running shoes to summer storms.
Souls and hearts wedded to the hills of Sapello.

Call the family, call a celebration,
from Los Angeles to Ponderosa scented forest.
Gather the neighbors to witness
what marries
all of us this day,
to what humans can know of the sacred,
the presence of the True Beloved.

From *What Marries Us*

THESE ARE THE BELLS, THE BELLS

that ring in the wind.
Hear how the bells sound across the plain of wind,
hammock of light.
A beautiful woman lies alone in the wind's music.
Rocking in emptiness,
swaying to empty.

And there is such a longing.
Even the wind stops to listen.

SLIPSTREAM

The moon comes up jingling
100 pieces of pirate's silver.

All bells sound, until they are lost.
They ring themselves past Venus,

and letters from my mother.

Her letters on pale silk paper,
drift down the Gallinas River, sad

as peaches,
caught in wild eddies.

I gather these letters,
tied with spider webs,

bound with honeysuckle.
I store them, pressed
in the collected works of Emily Dickinson.

Once in a dream, Cezanne saw them
but he thought they were apples.

Each bite was crisp with mother.
Each bite watches me carefully and will always.

Each bite was dangerous & loyal as goose love.

MARRIAGE IS NOT A PRETTY SUBJECT

Marriage is not table conversation.
And it's not clever.
Marriage is the third child, the fourth helping,
the fifth pair of red shoes.
It's too much of a good thing.

Marriage is pennies from heaven,
they sure add up slow.
Marriage is us at a movie.
Me wanting to leave,
you want to know how it ends.

Marriage is fried pork rinds and diet Sprite in bed.
It's the dog wanting out,
you pretending to be asleep.

Marriage is your prickly thighs
against mine. It's you kicking away the cat,
his returning to purr on my face.

Marriage is not a pretty subject.
Marriage is garden left on the garden salad.
Pushing pumpkin drawings out of the way to set the table.

Marriage is out of napkins,
using paper towel for tampons.
Marriage is three pairs of shoes under the couch,
none of them mine and I'm late.

Marriage is Kurt Gibson with his hurt leg,
in the bottom of the ninth,
first game of the '88 series,
hitting a homer off the A's that brings in three winning runs.
Marriage is the look on the A's pitcher's face
when he knows it.

Marriage is the look on Tommy LaSorda's face when he knows
    they got it,
running out of the dugout, hugging his boys and crying.
And that's why basesball is as good as art,
and marriage is as real as baseball any day.

ILLINOIS CENTRAL

It's a wife's job to be Joan of Arc.
You have to hear voices and follow them into battle.
You know you'll burn, you'll stand accused,
but you'll have seen God.

Seeing God is seeing baby ducks,
going by behind their mother,
slowly over waves.

If you look away they are farther than you thought,
But amphibian just the same.
Like angels, comfortable in three elements,
but frightened in the 4th way.

When God speaks
your only job is to listen.

Moses may have had a lisp,
but he knew to go barefoot on hallowed ground,
and when to shut up.

A wife has to be like Moses.
Her staff must turn into serpents,
her words into a plague of frogs,
and still know that quiet.
It parts seas, stops chariots.

A wife has to be Miriam,
the one whom the well followed.
Water has to follow her.
Her children drink when it is otherwise dry.
Can't you hear the westerly winds gracious in the tall grasses?
There is always moisture, the thrum of the tambor.
She knew if you crossed a sea, you better dance.

A wife needs relics, bones of queens, virgin martyrs.
She keeps them in labeled drawers,
wrapped in plain tissue, to dispense when needed.
To honor is her calling, her habit.

Her marriage must take sun like a turtle midday on the Rock River.
Take flight like the red wing blackbirds over starting corn.
Knee high in July, they say here.
She knows what that means.

Illinois makes her sleepy,
reminds her of saints and porch swings
that are always someone's mother's,
freshly painted every Spring.

Take the skiff out on the water.
She's sleepy, sleepy as a wife when the men talk,
and the wake rocks the reflected landscape
into a shakey dream of trees and sky.
She sleeps and doesn't dream.
She has been to the Mid-west, has heard voices
and thought, Fire Fire
I'm burning.

PRETTY GRIMM

Once upon a time she wore the pink high heels.
Wore them with the blue bikini in the summer kitchen.
A fly hissed around the ceiling fan.
The ceiling fan hissed a melancholy August swoon into the
    too hot room.
She stood, half in, half out of the refrigerator
Poised between cherries and Tom Collins in a glass pitcher,
    beaded wet
Poised between the sulky hot day in her house and that tidy cool.

There between the worlds,
a choice between ripe and reeling, and cooling down slow
Something was wrong.
Fee fi foo fum, you could smell the blood of

It wasn't about the ice box.
A mother is good about refrigerators.
They're full. Firm washed plums, tight skins ready to burst
The peaches mostly eaten,
pits left among the tart little grapes
lurking at the colander's starry bottom

It wasn't about the mirror
Every morning asking,
Who's the fairest of them all
Did she mean beauty or justice?

She has milk and bread, the mother in the blue bikini.
She has good rye, with chewy crusts, marigolds in her vase,
A surprise in the freezer, her black slip.
She might slip it on, shiver,
go out to corn and tomatoes ripening in the garden.

She is ripening too. The slip says that.
But the potato plant,
What does it say?

The radishes and beets say there is something underneath this heat.
Something growing that only the potato has eyes to see.

We need the spade and shovel in this story.

Take the shovel into the kitchen.
Dig up all the chocolate kisses for good mommies.
Throw them out.
Dig the deepest hole in the living room,
where the family gathers to pretend they are a family.
Dig it up. Unearth it all.
Rake in well, the hidden, the cool, the ripe, and the beckoning.
Will everyone live happy ever after?

DIVORCE AND TOASTERS

There's a calendar about my life.
It's saying "every other weekend" and "Thursday".
There's a season in my year, it's when hyacinth come up too soon.
But forsythia blooms even before that.

There's a clock that keeps ticking between my lover and his wife
and it says, "our house," and walks
walks on their land.

This is why my heart is like a garnet.
This is why my heart is not a ruby,
but semi-precious.

There is a toaster in my past.
The toast would pop up before it was done.
I'd spread it with butter as yellow as forsythia.
I used to have a blender, but I gave it away.
Divorced women need appliances.
Divorced women need clocks.

I used to have a table. It was set for four,
but I was never at my place.
The table says fork, spoon, knife.
I'm on the phone saying, "can't right now" and "maybe soon."
I call and say I'll call. "Later," I say, "later."

Later, the knife will appear at the child mediation hearings.
I take it into the courthouse,
but the guard takes it away.
"It's a butterknife, only a butterknife," I tell him.
I just want to show how domestic I really am,
I know what goes on the table.

I bring the toaster. I say, "See, I know about breakfast."
I was there for that.
But really, I only know enough about appliances
to unplug them before giving them away.

I only know enough about toast to say when it's done.
I only know enough about my lover
to put my heart back in the velvet box I keep in the top drawer
of the bureau that I gave away.

I only know enough about rubies to want one.
I only know enough about children to give them away.
I don't remember to unplug them.
I only know enough about tables to put the knife on the right.
I only know enough about forsythia to say butter and bloom.

There may not be Spring this year.
I gave it away.
My ex-husband got April, May, June and the kids.
I got the dog and the microwave, six plates and February.
I have a lover and he has a wife.
The forsythia hasn't bloomed yet,
but we know its color by heart.

No one has custody of my heart.
In mediation I give it to my lover, every other weekend and Thursdays.
I wear garnets to bed.
I'm a good lover, but I don't set the table.
I make toast under the broiler.
I have all my dresses shortened at the cleaners because I'm divorced.

Divorced women don't have blenders and do have lovers.
When I don't have the children, I can have strange men in my bed.
When I have strange men in my bed, I miss my lover and my children.
My lover misses his wife.
I miss forsythia blooming like clockwork and my ruby red heart.
My children miss me.
They have the toaster.

I set the table for two, for six, for one.
I'm practicing. I don't set knives.
I give them away for Valentine's day.
Every woman needs one.

Closed For Repairs

This marriage should be closed for repairs.
Lock the door, hang the sign.

CLOSED FOR REPAIRS
Call 988 et cetera for Further Information.

The number should ring to a machine that does 20 minutes of schtick,
and takes no messages.

> Yeah well, Jewish women like to take classes, it's our
> foreplay, Heidegger gets me so hot, ya know what I mean,
> So how's your weight, darling?...

On and on until you hang up, and I get back to business at hand.
Fixing this creaking, crumbling wreck of a marriage.

Maybe that's what I left in the back of the fridge.
Behind the salad dressing the kids hated.
The one I kept adding vinegar, then oil,
then vinegar, then oil.
'Til all I had was a lot of bad dressing.
Always too acid, too greasy.
Like Hansel and Gretel without the shove in the oven,
like Cinderella forgetting where in hell she'd left the other shoe.
Was it in her apron pocket, did she lend it to the birds?
Or left it, like this marriage,
in an undefrosted box in the kitchen.

Does the light go on, I wonder, when the door is closed?
Can I trick the light on, closing the door slowly?
Hang that sign, honey.
Closed for Repairs.

Now is the scene when the heroine walks in,
throwing caution to the winds.

Says, Hey lock that door!
Get wild! Say not one mean thought all day!
Fire the children! Let them get rehired as children tomorrow.
This marriage is open for repairs.
Let's talk about something that isn't us,
isn't old and worried like the dog's toys.
Don't fix one meal, tie one shoe.
Don't watch each other for the first slip up.
Let's talk about the Cubs,
April's first magpie,
where we'll put the corn patch.

Let's not get out of bed.
Let's try the dining room table.

Let's have a moment from a French movie,
Claude Lelouch with deep kissing and great lingerie.
Maybe a light rain.

Let's have a Western.
A John Ford,
where the man rides in, that's you,
and says, Honey, I'm here to fix this marriage.
Show me where it hurts.
Because it's a John Ford movie,
I will be Maureen O'Hara,
a stunning redhead with a teal ribbon barely holding my shining mane.
I will toss it and flounce around, and you will somehow
tame me without whooping or taking me down one peg.

We'll get in that wagon,
the one you built 2 scenes ago,
and we'll ride out in that sagebrush sundown.

Remember that sign that hung askew?
We'll turn it over.
It'll read, THIS MARRIAGE GONE WEST.

MEN NEED SPACE

Men need space.
We're talking South Dakota. Wyoming.
Men need Wyoming and the Mid-West.
The Mid-West was invented for men.
And it's a good thing, because women hate the Mid-West.
What's to like? The only good part is Chicago and moving away.
If Godzilla finally ate the place,
we'd only miss Seurat, Wrigley's Field and pizza.

The Cubs, my heartbreak team.
Only men and the Cubs can raise me to that perfect pitch
of eternal hope and utter despair.

It's like longing for Tzatziki in Santa Fe.
It's the Crusades, with just sand and no Grail,
A Matisse without blue.
Jane Austen minus drawing rooms and narrative structure.

Men make me stupid.
When my lover leaves I discover a burning need
to clean out my bathroom shelves.
I stop hiding the facial hair bleach.
I throw out all the lipsticks bought from $1 bins.
Peach, it turns out, is not my shade.
I'm an autumn, whatever that means.

I suspect it has something to do with men.
1000 monkeys would have written King Lear and the OED
long before figuring out the seasonal color theory.

Bookstores now have whole shelves about men.
The New Drumming Man. Men and Zen.
Men and Your Need for Orgasms. Men and Pain.
My question is, yours or theirs?

Women's magazines have always been about men.
How To Attract Men With Your Strong Yet Slender Thighs
How To Attract Men With Your Best Ever Chocolate Cake
Sheer Lacies With High Necks For That Lewd Yet Innocent Look
    Oh Baby

And Orgasms.

How To Have Them With Men
How to Have Them In Swiftly Moving Vehicles
Standing In The Shower
While Baking Best Ever Chocolate Cakes

Then there are books on how to live through the pain-on-wheels
due to feeding Best Cake with our devastating Thighs,
to these longed-for men.

Now we need meetings.
We need Co-Dependent No More Or Hardly Ever
At Least Seldom.
We need How To Love Yourself And Your Great Thighs More
While Mortifyingly Alone On Saturday Night

I had the best relationship of my life at Jewel-Osco.
I bought a bottle of Campari.
The club soda was right there at the cashiers.
I said to the Check-Out man, Now all I need is a lime.
Without missing a beat, he said,
Yes! And a cute guy to drink it with.
I said, Yes! And a Pre-Nuptial agreement.
He said, Yes! And a good divorce lawyer.
I said, Yes! I've been wanting to tell you I need....

And he said, Yes! We need to talk. I need space.

It was perfect.
We did the whole thing in three minutes.
I had recovered by the time I got to my car.

It spared us months of grief, enormous phone bills.
I didn't have to introduce him to my parents,
for whom he would never have been good enough.
His old girl friend didn't need to visit.

I didn't have to get my kids to like him,
he didn't have to work on my car.

Now, however, I'm in love.
Honey, he said, Darling, he said, I need space.
I felt sick.
He probably did not mean the Great Salt Flats.
Then he said the kicker, the clincher.
Sweetheart, it's not you.
Who isn't me? I ask.
You are not the reason I need space.
Who is, I say, my stomach dropping into my Tony Lama's.
Now, I'm dying.
I want to be the woman he needs space from.

Weddings and Armed Robberies

Being married is like a gun in your pocket.
It'll go off if you forget it's there.
Staying married is like stealing.
You need to make plans and tell them to no one.

I like weddings and I like stealing. I serve and get confused.
I want to be the bride.
Sometimes I want to be her sister.
Put a garland in her hair,
lend her my pearls.

Sometimes I do weddings.
Arrange tiny spring rolls on silver trays,
lay sprigs of fresh mint
beside salmon and chive cheese lavished
on slender pumpernickel rounds.
But my confusion may overcome me.
I'll pull out my paring knife,
raise my white neckerchief over my chin,
saunter up to the caterer, say,
This is a hold up, give me all your goat cheese rellenos.
I'll hold out my apron and fill it with crudites.
Gruffly, tell the wait people,
Shut your mouth and give me your dip.
I'll make the blonde that's my size strip,
and give me her black and whites.

Swaggering out the swinging door,
I circle correctly,
proffering my empty salver,
Give me your Rolex, I hiss sweetly,
and that glass of Dom Perignon '78.

The bride is so lovely,
my eyes fill with tears.
I always cry at weddings.
Throw the bouquet now, honey, I say,
The party's over, so sorry, hate to leave so soon.

The guests gather as they should.
She tosses the ribbon bound lilies and gardenias.
Without even trying, I gracefully catch it, left-handed.
I thank the hostess for a perfectly grand time,
head for the Bentley with Just Married on the hood.
I'll write, I promise, and I do.

Worst Sex

Darling, the worst sex award will be reserved for you.
And that's saying something.
Sometimes with my ex I'd wish I'd pasted Doris Lessing on the ceiling,
so at least I could impress other writers.
She is as boring as you.
Instead I'd lie there and plan the bakery schedule.
Grind, writhe, chocolate cake, thrust, moan, oatmeal
raisin, higher please, defrost
the butter. Arch, yes, more to
the right, muffins and tarts, pull out and plunge, lemon bread, god we
just made that, and we're already out.
Faster, now in, chocolate rum almond, panting, licking, gingerbread,
hands on, oh no, it's pay period, cash flow, cash flow.
All the way in, Friday
tomorrow, ooooooh, his eyes are rolling, we need challah.

But you. You hated me.
I'd love it and get so hot.
We'd lie in our damp bed in the Florida nights,
your eyes closed, I climb on top.
Never open your eyes, never touch me.
You loved tennis.
Lift, plunge down, ace a serve, slip back up, twist, great lob, back
arched, run to the net, got it.
It was love, love, love.

WHADDYA THINK IT MEANS?

The washing machine shakes violently,
Rocks, quakes and leaks.
It's moaning, a high pitched wail.
In mechanical I Ching it flashes:
       Unbalanced load
I know this.
Too much on the thighs,
too much on the brain, energy drained.
No money for land, food, clothes.
Hampered by debt and debit.
       Do Not Use
The change machine orders.
Does this mean I will always be the same?
I'm delicate, I protest,
I'm not a normal load.
My head spins,
no mercy in the Speed Queen today.

My machine is quirky.
My machine has a private and mysterious relation
to its function.
Put laundry in. The light says on.
It's a ruse.
Lurching, it spins dry and hard.
Then stops.
Then you add money.
Then it begins for real.

I only know this because the young woman who is my temporary,
instant laundromat friend,
tells me the secrets of this and other machines.
She has her own at home.
Hers is broken.
She had to walk. She has to walk back.

I become the Speed Queen shrink.
I help her remove telltale stains.
Blood, ink, wine.

I give her my All.
I drive her home.

I give the man taking his entire wardrobe
out of a black plastic bag, softener.
I explain the dryer in bad Spanish.
Pone dinero aqui, como esto es mas caliente, si,
vingt minutes, bien, suave.

I am the Lila Wallace of Laundry World.
I am building an audience.
We are increasing bi-lingual presentation skills.
We are benefiting contemporary awareness of storytelling.

But we do not need poetry.
We are in poverty.
We are in despair.
We need quarters and Purex.
We need Arm & Hammer, Wisk and Dash.
Perky verbs, and a brightener.
We need something safe for colors.

We do not need readings. We need someone to listen.
I listen to the machines,
rocking hard, squealing on their terrible axis,
'round an orbit of clean.

I seek cryptic Wisdom in the instructions:
This unit should not be used by children.
This unit will not operate with door open.
Do not Overload.
In case of mechanical failure,
Contact Trujillo's Liquor.

It may be too late.
We may be permanently pressed.
We've faded.
Worn out,
left on the line too long.

SCHOPENHAUER, HEIDEGGER AND A MORE SLENDER YOU

I hate my subliminal weight loss tape.
It's not subliminal at all.
I hear waves crashing in a gale force storm,
causing trees to fall on rooms where children are innocently sleeping.
The waves pound the shores,
and right between that ebb and pulse,
I hear a vicious old man, who is missing his uppers,
hokking and haranguing and insulting me and then I can't hear him,
then he's right there again, curmudgeoning and grumbling and the
waves are rising and destroying whole cities, priceless paintings,
     5000 years of culture.
You're fat and your grandchildren will be sons of pigs, he hisses,
and there goes Paris, the whole south of France, including all the
women with Bain de Soleil tans, and bathing suits that are just an
algebraic formula for straps.
Ugly, and you'll never lose thisss, you'll always look like a house,
surge crrrachkk, and fat and boom, stupid, seethe, doesn't and can't.
There goes Rome. All of Catholicism,
and trees are falling in forests, not silently,
not silently at all. I know, I hear them.

SOMETHING ABOUT DUCHAMP, LADY DAY, AND DANGER

Your sash about my sunflower waist,
and wasn't I always bending as if willow,
as if birch.
I called down the long stairs,
over the oak bannisters
to where the lovers were kissing, as in a dream.

His mouth on her eyes, and in her hair,
a white magnolia.

I could forgive them anything but that flower.

The exotic scent, the tissue creaminess of the petals.
There may have been a bruise,
I can't tell.

I went down and down,
breaking slowly into my tilted self.
A momentum of peel and shed,
until I was so much less,
only that bitter south of myself,
but nearly sweet,
as the milk of the red, red trumpet vine.

YOU'RE SO VAIN, YOU PROBABLY THINK
THIS POEM IS ABOUT YOU

Eleven headed Maitreya Buddha, dancing the cosmos into being.
In what way does this pertain to my childhood?
A Louis Sullivan cast iron baluster, a Robert Venturi
            Queen Ann chair,
Don't they just really remind you of me ?
Polynesian artifacts, the soft inner bark of mulberry, a kapa,
for bedding and burial.
Fascinating. They are just my taste.
They would be perfect for me.
Paddles, polished burl bowls for poi, Stunning.
So interestingly primitif, yet so, well, me.

I'm in my element.
And see that Liao Dynasty Quan Yin?
She reminds me exactly of my 4th grade teacher,
back in Duluth, wasn't it?
And that rainy Sunday, I ate raisins, six of them, on the steps of
the Methodist Church.

A seated Amida, Japan, 1700's.
That was that a good century for me.

Buddhism is about forgetting me, but only for one hall.
Not to worry, by Tibet we can start to think about me again.
And just in time too. This is a test.
You will be tested on me.
Which mudras best set off all my lovely rings?

A Jizo from the Kama Kura period,
Bodhisattva of wayfarers and children,
Avalokiteshvara, Bodhisattva of compassion,
Amazing.
14 centuries of devotional dharma is about my taste in statuary.

22

Krishna and Radha,
the folds of bronze drapery pooling into liquid dynamic.
Who could have guessed that Hinduism is also about me?
Me and my superb figure, me and the way green becomes me,
Me and how I take my coffee and how my boyfriend takes me.
Me and my tattoo.

There's a Don Flavin neon against the wall.
It's so technological. It reminds me of my car,
or is it my refrigerator?
How lights come mysteriously on.
Or maybe the toaster
How my life just pops up everywhere.

And look at that Archipenko, the play of open cubed space,
the sheen of the bronze.
So like the highlights in my hair, don't you think?
And the way I tilt my head,
Guess: Modigliani. My sense of humor,
Dubuffet.

BUTTON, BUTTON, WHO'S GOT THE BUTTON?

I'm safe because she doesn't know I'm here.
She's looking for me in Angel Fire.
She knows I'm a poet so she's looking for me in words.
She'll stay in present tense and try to kill me there.
I have to go back and back to where my mother is alive with a drawer
full of lapis and garnets,
and I'm eating Clams Rockefeller in a restaurant by a
lake with a cold man, but he kisses good.
He has another lover and she makes all her clothes.
She shows me the buttons of hand wrought silver.
The shirt is plaid.
I am safe again in a dream of wardrobe decisions.

Any detail can save me.
Buttons, and zippers, any closure is critical.

She is looking for me in her own story.
She moves into my house. My lover gives her my amber earrings.
It's a small price.

Today she has a switchblade.
Today she has a weight problem and an island of gangsters.
I'll have to be careful to get to my future.
I don't know the way. I'll sleep myself there.

I eat broiled chicken under the covers.
I have raspberry earrings and a rhyming dictionary.
She doesn't see me there, because I have the collected works
        of T.S.Eliot, and they make me molecularly diffuse.

My mother has a collection of photographs of crazy children.
That's just a dream.
I have that dream with a side of fries and the waiter says,
You need a half hour of sex and no habits.
You need a calendar minus this year.
You need to hide in fever because she'll find you in well.

You're usually there, it's a bad habit.

Even nuns don't have habits now.
God can't find you if you have a habit.
God looks for people in good clothes.
God likes a good dresser. Me too.
But she'll look for me in clothes.
I have to wear pajamas.

School days, school days, dear old Golden Rule days.
Nothing counts. Being good won't help.

She'll kill me with a baton.
She'll kill me with Homecoming.
She'll kill me with pep.
My side will lose.

She has a permission slip from her father.

She'll find me in America.
I'll die of the National Anthem.
I'll die at dawn's early light.
I'll wear stars and stripes forever.
She'll kill me with her inalienable rights.
She'll kill me with amendments.
She'll change my constitution.

She'll take the Fifth.
They'll repeal my right to bear arms.
I'll have no write to truth.
There will be no justice, now or ever.

I have the right to remain silent.
Anything I say
can and will be
held against me in a court of law.

SOMETHING ASHBERY TAUGHT US ALL

She watches the dust motes when you speak.
If you catch her eye it will unmake you.

You dread the unscrewing of the gummy lid.
You try to distract her with pasta al dente,
red wines almost acrid.
She never forgets to close the door behind her.
She calls often, leaves numbers.

You cream your feet, apply lipstick, eat blood oranges.

You test the water for heavy metals.
You wake in the night, heart pounding.
You have no symptoms.
Your condition worsens.

She is permanently cheerful.
She is concerned how you slept,
how your day went.

She has your unopened mail in her top dresser drawer,
beneath soiled handkerchiefs.
She keeps a small gauge pistol for the emergencies you never see.
You weren't there. You couldn't know.
She tells you it wasn't your fault.

You slip down the fine oil of her glance.
She spreads over you.
A thin film you can't bear to touch.
You bathe daily in lavender salts, but you still smell medicinal.
There is no cure.

You rub her in, a liniment.
Your heels dry and crack, no matter what.
She calls to remind you to take your temperature.
She is your fever, you flip your pillow,
seeking the cool side.

We Cannot Find What is Not Lost

Death comes from miles away.
I see it coming towards me, double barreled.
A drum, a drum beat humming,
Belly dancer of death, the seven veils lifting off.
John the Baptist, you lonely old waiter,
dipping yourself into the blood waters of Judea.
Over and over, asking everyone:
Are you my master, Are you my master?

You wound up served on a platter yourself, old prophet,
for the whims of a silken shrouded woman,
Salome, who called for your head,
As if any one man's death can end the search for the great teacher.

PAULA'S STORY

1.
It was when
he smoked that first cigarette on the trestle over Rock River
pissing down laughing
getting high and sick

and Jimmy Spergus told them around
the second, or third, bottle how his father
at every family gathering
told about the eldest daughter
Paula who jumped
off the silo in their wheat field
and was never seen again, they said aw that

old story, jeezus you've told that one
a hundred times, what do you mean never seen
again? He said well there was no one around and she just
sailed off that silo, never hit the ground,
they searched the corn through and that
is the truth. And my Dad swears up and down it was
terrible how they missed her, it's what happened.

II.
When I fell
it was not like the Reverend said,
not a descent to hell
but a pure fall, and falling still.

Father says I'd lose my head
if it weren't screwed on,
slow as winter molasses, a butt
full of lead.

That June I began dropping
Mother's good glasses, the plates
from her mother, I had to see
if the ground could stop them.

By harvest time I knew
that what is real cannot land.
From our silo's top, looking
out into an unreaped blue,

Too blue, too tempting, down
below the fields with singular
golden bales, tied and ready
I planned to make no sounds

As I leapt, but I did wonder
who would hear, or come
running off the white porch,
the rocker rocking dumb.

Heart is Where the Home is

"If you ever visit this island,
he'll grow you back to your
childhood".
John Ashbery

You never left.
Palm fronds blew in a Southeasterly breeze.
Snakes hissed, but you never saw any the whole time.
I don't see old lovers and I don't see snakes, you said.
Look, she said. You don't.

When the rains came, you went walking.
Butterflies came out in a rain forest, green the color of poison.
And the way the light slanted in.

You were small. They called and called.
You didn't show yourself until much later.
By then you had read the books.
You were nobody's fool.

At dinner you cleaned your plate.
After, there was always the closet, and the door slightly ajar.
And that spear of light.
Or maybe it was the hush of the fanblades,
the tinkling of the chain pull.
You never knew. No one asked.

They assumed you were safe because you were small.
You never stayed long.
Every morning you walked out into dense undergrowth
        behind the house.
And then the part about the butterflies again.

You never told anyone.

Why should you?
Everything matters.
The Koi in the pond were flashing orange, the color of alarm.

Everyone said they cared.
At night you read long after midnight.
You never finished a book, each one carefully closed with 8 pages left.
It's better that way, you said. Clearer.

You won't go back there. Ever.
Who could blame you?
It was only a place. And those butterflies over and over.

Knives of light
The sound of rain overhead.
Or was it the fan, going round and round?

Shadows were spaced evenly on your bed.
Why should you weep? You didn't.

You drank rainwater. Read on, went for walks, spared no one.
Not even me, not even yourself.

You'll never visit. You know no one.

4:00 and the slanting storms.
Sun through palms, green as snakes you never see.
Everything matters, even the butterflies.
Even the golden light.

You don't hesitate.
It wouldn't be right.
You'd take your life in your hands.
Any one would.

THE SORRY OF FLOWERS

A dark horse ambles slowly through my apology.
A field of alfalfa and wild columbine,
I'm that sorry.
I'm sorry in the way of going too soon to seed.
I'm sorry in the way of haste and meadows,
a season of sorry, a harvest of regret.

But there's that animal in me that is not sorry.
That has moved with mysterious resolve
towards insult and mayhem.
That is maybe a bit gleeful,
accelerating to a brisk trot,
Then full tilt gallop,
a whirr of black behavior.
Unforgivable!

Sweet Honey of Refusal

The No burning all the way down.
And me, living on codeine and marsh birds.
Least Bittern and Curlews.
Grasslands of sorry and never.
Slipping sideways to disappear,
masters of alarm and gone.

I wasn't promised more. I admit it.

That wasn't the mistake.

It was the slovenly wanting.
An accident of desire, a careless moment of need.

Now, learning again, as a toddler does,
by falling.

Holding back wanton.
Not like the bees.
Even the drones in a drunken, servile
haze of pollen, believing.

Take Caution Caution Caution

Meadow birds, the red under one wing hidden,

magpies, their iridescence seen
from one sudden view.

Swift wings over Cattails, pills and regret.
Kingfishers clinging to high wire.
It's hard to sway on such taut belief.
Yet they manage.

Sorrow suddenly electric, humming downline.
You could run the canyon on grief tonight.

Dip and dive, beside Plovers and Mergansers,
plunging beneath the icy ribbon of wave
for what they know will feed.

I can't know anything.

That ruffled surface,
silky, green,
will suffice.

Dropping down into that sweet demise,
No, no no no said over and over.
Such honied failure,
such cold return to air.

10,000 WAVES IN SHOJI TUB

Writing
In the damp and steam, the pinon turn bonsai.
Heat in puffs rising towards a paper lamp,
shaped like something in Japanese I haven't the character for.

And the cedar deck laid in with such precision,
saying order and attention, detail.

It's so decent, junipers drop
recent rain
under a clouded sky.

Heat rising, letters. Fresh scent.

Rainy days were for arts and crafts in summercamp.
We went through a Johnson pine forest,
needles thick as a bed
underfoot.

Rain was the smell of the walk to copper enameling,
the yellow slickered, red rubber boot trek
to press leaves between wax paper.
Small girls, heads down, in a line, march towards the smell
of white sweet paste to cement popsicle sticks into boxes
with lids that come off.

My children make boxes of these popsicle sticks at home,
They glue them into gifts for me, as I once did.
The lids are also removable.
They are gifts for the removable mother.
The mother who goes on and off,
is perhaps in the woods,
is perhaps on the rainy road home.

ACCIDENTAL POETRY

I lie in bed and take pills.
I feel like Frieda Kahlo, except I can't paint.
When everything hurts, the world becomes vivid.
The seconds go off like automatic weapons.
I want to invent clouds, make a humidity to coat me.

My legs remind me just exactly of green gold Macaws.
Just exactly.
I could try on pairs and pairs of beaded earrings in this mood.
And none would be right.
I want red, red lipstick and blue eyeshadow.
I need a beauty mark above my lip,
and a cruel lover who holds my wrists down.

I am flagrant. I am nearly interesting.
There's a certain weather to it, sticky and damp.
I play music from the Mexican Revolution.
Viva, I keep saying, Viva.

I spend hours in the bathtub. I'm fine, I say.
I say it in Spanish for effect.
I would try on black lace anything.
I need to have an affair,
drink old wine,
and paint that green that is only in jungles and broken bodies.

***

When you write a poem,
some lines will be the best you ever wrote,
and some will be the worst.
Is the same true of car accidents?

Was this my best one, or my worst?
Is the same true of clouds,
And are my thoughts as slow as photosynthesis because of pain?

In another dream, my shoulder has pierced my skin
and is exposed to air.
The bone is white, like a good beach.
I lie there, still as nothing ever is in wind.

***

The clouds float by in a sky real as glass.
There was glass between my teeth, glass everywhere.
The Angels had beautiful red dresses
and they could sing like the Supremes.
Stop in the Name, they sang.
They offered me dinner.
I can't, I said, I'm busy.
Can't you see I'm having an accident?

It was fried chicken, my favorite.
But I said, uh-uh.
I want to ride in the ambulance now.
I want my heart to stop and maybe my breath.
My pulse flickered yes, no. Yes, no.
The Angels said, But we made gravy.
No, I say, I have a craving for risk.
A yen for crisis.
I have the gift of disaster.

See how I never scar.
See how my skin, clear as a lampshade, shines.

You could make book on my survival.
But there's good odds.
It's that close.

My vital signs are stable.
It's another miracle, Angels and all.

When the world stopped, the radio was still on. A car stopped.
I was caught in a windy future.
Heart of darkness, heart of glass.
I wrestle with Angels, saying Stay, and Please.

Like Jacob, I watch the ladder.
Is there a Temple near here, I ask.
I am hurtling through space at the speed of catastrophe.
I am a one woman calamity.
I'm something I can't prevent.

I invented the wrong story,
And I have to write the end only this one way.

***

The clouds float by in a sky real as glass.
There was glass between my teeth, glass everywhere.
When the world stopped, the radio was still on. A car stopped.
I said, I'm hurt, very bad. Take me to John's house.

Papers were blowing everywhere,
My poems were roaming the night like loose women.
The only sound in the night was static.
I wanted to keep breathing but it hurt so much.

I said, Please, my poems are all over the road.

The only sound in the night was sirens.
I'd done it this time.
The real metal and glass thing.

I lay down on the road next to my poems.
I was calm and wanted to keep breathing.

I veered toward truth
And she met me head-on.

***

My sister has a new formica counter.
But I get to have accidents. Look Ma, no hands!
She re-papers the dining room, a small print,
Laura Ashley, it goes with the teak Danish Modern.

I take codeine with white wine, then I sleep.
My mind creeps like a toddler.
This is a game where the first sister to lose everything wins.
Guess who wins?

I'm on the phone, trying to tell her,
Nancy, I'm, I mean, how the road, I was, the curve Nancy
She is telling Scott's mother where his blue shovel is.
Karen, she is saying, Look in the sandbox
She tells her daughter, Honey, Mommy will be off the phone
    in a minute.
Let Mommy talk to Aunt Judy. Yes you can
and save the rest for after dinner
I'm saying, Nancy, the car, Nancy

***

The clouds float by in a sky real as glass.
There was glass between my teeth, glass everywhere.
When the world stopped, the radio was still on. A car stopped.
The night road to Galisteo was glittering, glistening,
singing towards me as fast as everything gets better in a TV
    marriage.
I am tumbling towards an inescapable conclusion.
I am confused as a bad plotline,
Predictable as sit-com.

It's unavoidable, a destiny of crack-up and broken glass.
The sounds of radio wavering into the night.
The swift rolling, a tumult,
A river of metal moving downstream over rocks,
in a valley of next times.

Are bodies meant to hurtle in space, fast as science?
Quixotic as a paradigm.
So this must be the Quantum Leap.
What cats know about landing,
I know about falling.
What Einstein knew about later,
I know about right now.

I crawl from the crushed heap.
There is no other way to say this.
Nothing got better in thirteen years.
I tried and tried.
There was broken glass everywhere,
You just couldn't see it.

Believe this. I crawled out.
I promise you I was on my knees.
I said, I'm hurt, very bad. Take me to John's house.

CODE BLUE

A poet is not a nurse, but a wild thing.
Her mind is a box full of violets and rare metals.
Her heart is a fakir's bed.
You have to believe this doesn't hurt.
She has a dictionary of the uses of sharp objects.
The 12 steps to forgetting.
She hasn't a white uniform.
She hasn't shoes that squeak.
She has lyrical lines but no bedside manner.
She is faithful as the night sky, which is to say, seasonal.
Which is to say darkness and light.
She carries planets in her brain cells,
whole galaxies in her DNA.
She will not be nice to you.
She does not care if you get better.
She has a mouth full of bad weather, teeth full of storm.
She leans out the windows of 3 story walk-ups,
says, come up.
You haven't a prayer.
There are aisles in her bathrooms, clocks in her refrigerators,
when the light goes on, they tell you the time in Bosnia, Kuwait
and Somalia.
She has a digital readout of statistics you don't want to know.
Her calendar shows the day Charlie Parker blew his sax all night at
125th and Lenox.
And the IRT rattled by under the grates, while a gust of warm air
rises under Marilyn's skirt, Castro visits Manhattan, the cops beat up
her sister in Union Square, the Dead play Fillmore, Fellini makes
Amacord. It's when Neruda writes 100 love poems. Duchamp's Nude
descends the Staircase.

Her brain never shuts up.
Her brain writes Pulitzer prize winning novels in Spanish while she
sleeps. She wears absolutely nothing to bed.
Can you bear it? Would you love her?

She listens to The Eroica, and brushes her hair.
Whole countries fall apart.
Mushrooms grow under fallen wood in Alsatian forests.
She wants everything marinara.
She wants to learn German and already know astronomy.
She fakes constellations.
She hates horses and novels where bad things happen to children in
the first fifty pages. Everything matters.

She drinks only Riesling and bourbon.
If you come to dinner, you will be sorry.
She is sultry as Joabim and overwrought as Poe.
A flat, E, C, C minor, A.
A jazz rift forms like a tidal pool.
Crabs scuttle like Eliot's old ghosts.
But she never sees them, she hasn't the attention span.
Her mind's two thoughts away.

She's not nearsighted but has her focus on Flaubert, on Venice,
on Carrara marble, on bestiality, on red silk stockings,
on elaborate desserts too exhausting to bake.
Proceed at your own risk.
There are corridors in her basement.
The super is banging on her pipes,
and the young arty couple below her whack her ceiling with an
upraised broomstick. When is she quiet anyway?
She is eating toasted seeded rye bread with thin slices of cheddar.
Butter drips through the places where it isn't bread.
She plays Mahler 5th. Loud. Von Karajan's version.
She'll give you mouth-to-mouth and you'll wish you were drowning.
She wears coral kimonos, and writes letters to dead poets.

Dear Sylvia,
Saw Ted with that awful co-ed again. Ariel is the greatest thing
you've ever written, and The Bell Jar is the worst. Worms like sticky
pearls is a fabulous line, Sylvia, fabulous. Why didn't you wait
two more hours?

The best part of the city is the docks,
but it's not because of ships, as much as sailors.
They leave and leave. They wear white and dress alike like brides.
They are special, like good dolls.
She has the house.
She has a couch and a tea set.
She is a doll that wets and cries real tears.
She is expensive, with real rooted hair.
You'll pay what she's worth, she'll inject you with nothing.
Your prognosis is tenuous. It could go either way.
You'll pay and pay.
You'll get exactly what you paid for.

Life is a Series of Events That Seem Important at the Time

Workshops couldn't have taught Hemingway how to write.
He'd be lying on his back
visualizing the declarative sentence expanding into space,
moving downtown over Thanksgiving's 79th street while
For Whom the Bell Tolls floats unmoored, high overhead, uptown.

Joyce would be practicing shorter line lengths and snappy repartee.
He'd be on his way to Advanced Editing
while Ulysses passes him on the other
side of narrative structure, head down, deep in thought.

Tolstoy would be working on his resume and sending out query letters.
The samovar would hiss.
He'd sip and through the smoke miss Anna's leap into the tracks,
and we'd never know why she did it, why.

Jane Austen would do custom-tailored Armanis and lunch at Spago.
The buzz on the Rodeo says she's doing a new screen-play for De Niro.

Shakespeare would have gone to acting school and wound up a waiter.
Fitzgerald would have become a male model,
and then the shipping director for Mercedes Benz.
He'd have died sadly sane on the right side of the Atlantic.

Poe would have stayed Poe.
Even a binge of creativity classes
couldn't have swayed his collision course with literary calamity.

Emily Brontë would have joined Al-Anon,
and moved to a climate with more sun.
Women would be forced to meet Heathcliff
in an endless stream of terrible relationships
they'd never understand.

It's writing re-hab.
Your characters will contract terminal diseases in secret.
You'll lose your voice, manuscript and your advance,
Wind up with a day job, time on your hands.

No Later

You must change your life, the poet wrote.
Forget artist's angst.
Even Delphi, even Constantinople.
No Temple can hold your prayers now.
This is the later you were waiting for.

Get off your knees and run.
Say Boruch, say Salaam, face cardinal North.
Turn the compass toward Mecca.
Make a new truth in Somalia, Kuwait and T cells.

Get the Generals out of the story,
and put the particulars in.
Get out of your journals and into the newspaper.

Don't let another day go by, the poet wrote.
Tell us the hot, sweet swirl of Darjeeling on your tongue.
The smell under your lover's arm after carving,
hair curling tender on his chest.

Visit Matisse at the Met, Monet at the Modern.
Walk the sidewalk in your hometown. Step on all the lines.
Don't be careful. Be loud in restaurants.
Send orchids and day lilies to the one who returned your long look.
Insist on trees. Remember your dreams.

Open your mouth your door your beliefs.
Drop a pin. Hear silence. Hear Neruda sob like the moon
in a pocket of sky. Sprinkle like salt.
Cry, said the sculptor Naranjo, and live.

YOUR WRITING'S NOT IN COCHITI

Not at the dam,
where the ring-tailed lemur hunts among dark granite.
Not by the lake, where the mallards dip and dive.
It's not by Buckman Reservoir,
no matter how high the Rio is running,
how sedimentary and Zen the river rocks are.

Your writing's not in the Gila.
Not bathing in 7 successive pools of hot springs,
ringed by mysterious grottos.
You'd light a candle and pray if you could.
But you can't because you've left,
to sit in a cowboy bar in Silver City,
drinking too much Turkey,
listening to songs about losing your job, your love and your dog
& waiting for your writing.

But writing stands you up again.
So you head for the Bosque.
Your writing isn't there, but 7 eagles are.
It's January, and there are Sandhill cranes and the 13 Whoopers.
They've forgotten their courting dance and you have too.
You watch their spindly long legged grace.
Knobby knees and bobbing walk.
Their innocence stuns you.

Watch them through binoculars.
It's so idyllic. It's so inspiring.
You'd write about them.
But your writing's in Socorro,
Eating a fiesta omelette, drinking bad coffee at Jerry's Diner.

The busboy's shaking his ragmop and glaring.
And the waitress, whose boyfriend just dumped her, is wiping her tears
and forgetting the toast.
You're just pulling in, as your writing takes off north.
You order hot chocolate,
the kind they make with water, and ponder maps.
The biscuits are plump and real. You plan a trip.

You'll take your typewriter.
You'll be quiet. You'll be alone.
You'll have time.

Meanwhile your writing's in Santa Fe.
Writing's taken your old job & gotten a raise.
Writing's dating your ex
and meeting your friends at the Grand Illusion Cinema.
Writing's eating popcorn with real butter and brewer's yeast,
just the way you like it, as the house lights dim.
Your mother's calling writing.
Your father sends money & offers of downpayments.

You're trying to figure out
if you should live up in the Jemez without electricity.
Your writing's buying new red Tony Lama's and a cappuccino maker.
Your writing's got it good.
Sitting in your kitchen, sipping espresso,
looking out your window.

A Plot Calling the Characters Back

I wanted to write the perfect short story. Poets always do, secretly. We imagine the words that go all the way across the page. The ones we don't say. I wanted a story with strong narrative thrust, a woman on her hands and knees, moaning in ecstasy. I set it out West, with an aging, warm/cool Willie Nelson type, whose fiery, and yet deeply decent, wife of many years (who's let her career go to be Mrs. Willie) warns off the up & coming young blonde thing on the road tour. Of course the blonde on the move thinks it's ridiculous, she's gonna Have It All. So wifey shoots her. I would have.

But it had too many pronouns, played like an overwrought Made For TVer and kept ending too fast. I added a train, a tunnel, a dining car. There was a pink rose budding in a silver vase, a view of the snowy peaks of the Alps, and the stiff little shade pulled down on the sleeper window at just the right.... It read like Hitchcock, and I'd lost the firearms in my first story in the truck stop shooting, because Christina had thrown the .38 behind the rear view mirror and windshield defoggers on aisle 4. That left a greening hillside, scudding clouds and a feisty red-head cooking steel cut oats for her brothers, wishing for her man and a parlor for doin' her mendin' of an evening. He would sit by the fire. Later, chores done, she'd play the spinet. This story had a tea cozy, scones, clotted cream and tenors. It was all dairy and dreamy, a brogue, a pub, dark beer and fair-haired daughters, Fiona, Bronwen and Lily. But it kept ending in a mine disaster, that whistle and weeping, widows. The sons in bitterness burying their fathers & quitting school to work.

I tried India, but my mind went blank in a haze of sandlewood incense and the hiss of cobras. I smelled dust and white brahmas, cows and nuns and cardamom. There were temple walls carved into the multi-phenomenal mating of Shakti and Shiva, and the deep lotus foot of the Buddha. But maybe that was Japan. No, there were no cherry blossoms in sight. Just gurus and ashrams, boddhi trees and then desire and another 1000 years of karmic attachment. It was exhausting. Besides, I couldn't stop it from turning Colonial, Englishmen in immaculate white linen suits drinking gin and bitters in air conditioned clubs, sunk down in deep leather armchairs, full of I say old chap, and the latest cricket scores already two weeks old, and face it, it had been done.

My story waited patiently, in need of a white '65 T-Bird convertible, a tough minded brunette, a .44, a breakfast of fried eggs over easy with a side of home fries, a cuppa Joe. The door of the cafe swings open with a squeak and in walks Vincent Van Gogh. I can't help it. I told him he was in the next story, and it started one page later, but he was hysterical and impatient and demanded absinthe and a plot. The light turned up 100 kilowatts. Everything, the kat clock, the yellow formica table tops, dissolved in a crisp of crazy and too loud. The light of Arles burned through the scene, like nitrate film bubbling from the center towards the edges, taking the soundtrack, in a hiss, at the end.

EXCUSES TO HAVE SEX

I have excuses to have sex.
It's your hand, your mouth, and your way of lying next to me
with all our good parts touching.
Your hand on my waist is operatic.
How can I keep from breaking into a sweat, into an aria,
into the opalescent blues of Renoir,
when your touch shines through me.
They could name a school of painters after us.
Hand me a palette.
I'll paint you excuses to have sex,
an ecstasy of water lilies that you don't have to step back to see.

My darling, I don't need excuses to have sex.
You and I are my excuse.
We are the Elizabethan period. Sonnets in motion,
14 lines, iambic, dactyl.
We're the Ming dynasty in vases, the Etruscan of jugs.
We're Hank Aaron, a record in home runs,
Annapurna and the Nile, a full flood plain.
We're hot crayfish and cold beer.

I don't need excuses for sex.
I only need you to explain the thought process of whales,
the nine words for waterfall in Japanese, Picasso's later
work in concrete, what Goethe told Emerson.
I don't need an excuse when your breathing changes
to short and fast from deep and long,
when you move towards me.
I didn't know my days could begin this way,
in a fever of desire,
the morning light rolling in, tender,
on two bodies, in love, in heat,
with no excuses necessary.

There's No Way to Love Without Being Changed

I am a woman of fevers.
A woman who rises to degrees past safety and goes
    all the way through.

Loving you has taken me into the danger zone of heat,
to a place on the dial of red zone, reading,
"Call the repairman when the needle reaches this line."

I walk that line with all my heart.
I call no one for help.

I am not the same woman who couldn't bear to look at your
dark beauty.
I am a woman of rivers now.
Can take any waters to your door,
and always enter your arms like an Amazon traveller,
like Henry Hudson finding New York,
like Magellan finding China.
I sail straight to the juiciest part of you
and all winds rush to my cause.

I am a woman of beauty who dresses for dinner.
Who wears silk scarves and perfume
and sheds her clothes like trees lose leaves,
in joy, in color.

I am not the same as before I put my mouth on yours
and knew poems would come of it.

I am a woman of heat and rivers,
and I enter your life in a rush of
hot and wet and willing.

No More Tears For Africa

Freedom cries out from all corners of the world.
And in my corner,
Purple irises on my lover's table.
I see them and know.
As if this was a Chinese poem, he is sleeping.
As if this was simple, he has loved another.

In Czechoslovakia, elections are held,
But will I ever see their delicate, hopeful way with Spring?
In South Africa's morning light,
Nelson Mandela sits over his breakfast in a cafe. It's simple.
It's as if a poem had set him there, stirring cream into his coffee.

I wanted to write about choosing to act, and call it:
                No More Tears for Africa.
I wanted to write a poem about response
and tell you that responding is a prayer.
It's praying to support the good —
To hold the world towards what is good.

The irises go off in my poem like an alarm.
I take one and press it in my journal,
as if grief was a place I only once read about,
but didn't want to live there.

I wanted to say, "No More Tears for Africa,"
as if it was a fact, a response, news.
But the irises taught me this prayer:

        Let us cry more tears for Africa,
And tears for the bloodied bodies of children.
        Bless the children
Whose pictures hang in living rooms
        Where the sound of their play no longer rings.

Let us cry more tears for America
And tears for plutonium sites.
   Bless Los Alamos and the scientist,
His heart hardened like a pharaoh against us.
   Let him see there is no Egypt now,
It's all promised land.
If the Red Sea closes, it closes on us all.

   Let us cry more tears for the flocks of snow geese,
Deep in the wild heart of the Bosque.
   Blessed is the tender flight of the redwinged blackbird.
Help us to know that we are the stewards
   of the heron, the meadowlark, the cot,
The WIPP Route and plutonium triggers.

   Blessed is Ghost Dance Fault
Where once the fierce Paiute danced for all the people.
   We ask blessing for Rocky Flats, for Carlsbad,
May we never say their names,
   that we do not see the great flocks wheeling overhead,
      and remember
                                        Amen.

We choose,
Over and over, to feel grief instead of numb,
for students clubbed in Tiananmen Square.
Over and over, we choose to feel horror instead of denial
for the water cannons pointed against small bodies,
in the dark streets of Soweto.

We choose, every day, we awake and choose speech
      over silence
for the radioactive mistakes of America.

Over and over, we choose

No More Tears for South Africa,
I wanted to tell you.
But there are tears. It's very simple.
Like a poem I will keep choosing to write.
Like the purple irises in the clear vase,
I'll sound an alarm,
and it will ring for freedom
From all the corners.

We will awake and pray:
    No More Tears
                   Amen

THE REAL REVOLUTION (IS EVOLUTION)

This morning I woke knowing Marx was wrong.
History isn't the dialectic of class struggle.
History is waking up beside you so many mornings.
History is knowing how your feet feel on mine,
as the coffee's darkness starts us.

I am a student of history:
I have an M.A. in You.
My speciality? Jurassic. You and I and dinosaurs.
You and I discovering electricity with Tesla.
Goethe called us to read The Second Poem The Night Walker Wrote,
right after he finished it.
And Coleridge? Did we leave him lonely too often?
If we had just sent him those few extra pounds,
he would have finished Kubla Khan.
But you bought me irises, blue irises, my love.
That is history.

BIRTHDAY BUOYANT

For John

44 candles and I count myself lucky.
The full measure of Chanukah and more.
My own yearly miracle of light, you roared
into yourself on this day,
at the base of a mountain, swaddled in mist
chortling quixotically in Japanese
or did they find you in a Shinto temple,
the monks
silently carving Buddhas in your honor?
I know I do. On this day,

Still shining, an answer to my prayers
for a paramour of fire.
A thousand cranes blessed,
An arrow flying straight to the heart of desire.

For 44 circlings of sun and unnumbered more
in this bow of grace
I cross my fingers, uncross my legs,
and hope to live.

LITTLE AMANDA TALKS TO THE MOON

Little Amanda kicked her heels,
O Ha'penny moon, said she,
I read by your light, which you borrow from day,
And nary a care have I, have I, nary a care have I.

O little Amanda, the Children's moon called,
Come play on the swings today!
Tilt your chin towards my face, and reach for the trees.
Tickle the tops of the leaves, the leaves, Tickle the tops of the leaves!

Little Amanda pointed her toes,
And said to the Gibbous moon,
You shine as if you meant it,
And were a bright and silver spoon!

Well, Miss Amanda, the moon said, yearning,
It's for your advice that I am burning.
A quarter slice more and I am turning.
Will I then be full?

O Moon, you ask the silliest riddles,
Amanda said and swung her legs straight to the sky.
I long to go higher, and higher and higher,
Then I'll know you why.

Amanda, my Janer, the Full Moon laughed,
Come dance in my light and discover,
The secret of ships and orange pips,
And whether butterflies laugh and cry, whether the butterflies cry!

Indeed my Moon, Amanda said,
As she swung up into the blue,
You'll disappear, and leave me here,
With only a trail of stars, of stars, a milky trail of stars.

I'll never leave you, Manda, my girl,
The big round moon replied,
I'll only go dark, and you are the spark,
That relights me from afar, afar, relights me from afar.

Where Water Has Been Recently

So have I.
Walked the aspen meadows so full of wildflowers this year.
Gentian that wait 30 years, bloom now.
Throw themselves to pale green petals, spotted, feline.
Field orchids, those showoffs,
doing color tones in a diatonic scale of violets,
the Charlie Parker of buds.
Sun cats move up the steep slopes to mineral pools,
and the heat, in waves,
smoke, scarves, curls down the mountain
like tears along the groove between nose and cheek.
A mountain cries, like men cry.

This year I'm studying men and wildflowers.
Their radiance astounds me.
It's about rain, and the heart's water.
Fields flung to Indian Paintbrush, that slut of a flower,
putting out all summer.
Rowdy next to the demure bells of the Yucca.
And how I opened the sweet purple edged blossom,
revealed the inner creaminess, the blatent stamen.
Holding there bravely for all to see.
Soapy smell, clean, baby after a bath.
The backs of the petals, the color of bruise.

But there's no rage in flowers.
The Tamerisks hold all stages of bloom at once.
From tiny mild white balls to full pinky spikes.
It's so matrimonial,
and the smell, a Westchester backyard at sunset.
There might almost be fireflies.
Instead there were eagles.
Men are too big for mason jars.

We walk through the virgin Aspen in an Arizona forest.
All around us, the erotic sheen of green,
the fragrance of wild strawberries, an echo of past roses.

You and I and Steve wonder how elk can run through dense woods,
and not lose their antlers.
I stop, alone, and study the dense trees.
Suddenly I find the way of elk through brush.
They don't see the trees, I say.
They see the spaces between.
Now we know the secret of antlers.
And I know a secret about men.
They are watching the spaces.

I watch you two. Beloved men.
Your velvety bodies, sun darkened and hard with work.
Calm with each other.
Deep in your talk and friendship.
A grove, not for women to enter.
I am laughing.
Whatever I thought beautiful before was a rehearsal for this moment.
Warriors, Lovers, Kings.
Men, beaming with the many petaled, verdant energy,
wounded, various,
rare.
Complex and mysterious as any orchid,
a swath of life, wet, rich, sweet
as where water has just lately
been running.

WHAT YOU ALREADY KNOW

Love me in that darker place tonight.
Not the place where men and women wage war,
but that other, the deeper pocket,
A valentine of velvet, not of lace.
Cave where owls cry, whooo, whooo
and I never know the answers to that question.
Spend it all, save nothing for a rainy day,
there might not be a later in this story.
You're the beloved I asked the Elephant God for,
when I said I could bear anything for love,
I meant it.

I knew it would be your night sweetness, that bitter taste,
the backdoor of the heart.
There's a window in this loving,
I look out and see you carving the tender meat of stones
into the forms every god loves.
Kali could dance to you,
Krishna and Miriam and the Cornwoman chant you.
A circle of animals move around a fire ring in Tent Rocks,
Sleek panther and the wild eyed bobcat.
It was our cathedral. You kissed me there.
Under a boulder held tight in a niche above our heads.
I sat with you.
It was all the safety you could offer. I accepted.

BEING AS HOW

my hair falls softly over your chest,
beloved, I reach for you.
It's the quiet of the familiar.
A walk I have taken many times and know each turn
in that September wood, where summer's weeds lie thick and fallen,
Russian olives, their branches bare
save for a few stray berries.

I look into your eyes and see my own dark ones.
Call to you from separate hillsides,
and find you beside me.

It's another season.
The trees leaf out, silver,
an alacrity of life, branch and bud.
Each stage is one that does not predict the next.

I'm Cupid. I'm Psyche.
No one holds a candle to you.
I practice the archery of love.
Send arrows of praise to your belly,
the tender curls of hair, there and lower.

I'm not alone, but sit separate and writing.
You are making dust of mahogany, of delicate ash,
of speckled granite from New Hampshire forest.
You know the woods like I know your body.
By memory, by heart.

By this I want to say matter.
What matters between us.
The way my body is resilient under yours.
The undertow of quiet in the deep of night.
We sleep under the same blanket, the same stars.
Constellations spin and we breathe,
held in the matrix of Pleiades and talk.

It's architectural.
We've made this bridge in the piney scented forest.
In this constant conversation,
on the edge of our seats, enrapt.

What Marries Us

For Randy and Jane, August 13, 1994

Each to each other,
his kids to hers,
her sexy grey braid to the way he loves whales.
It's all in the soup now,
a great fragrant pot, muy delicioso,
that can bring all of us through any winter.

What marries
the white stones of St. John's to blue waters off Okinawa.
It's divine, it's no accident,
It's the love they practiced for.
What marries us, taking love vitamins,
testing the muscle for commitment.

Lift the veil, make a vow.
Let the bluebells ring.
Know what marries us, each to each other,
every day saying over and over.
We do, we will,
saying, for richer and richer,
in our health and yours.

It's an honor
to share what marries us,
late night romance to diapers,
running shoes to summer storms,
Souls and hearts wedded to the hills of Sapello.
Groom the horse, throw a bridle on,
and canter off, into the vega, knee deep
in wild roses, purple asters,
the green grasses of August,
a ripening future of alfalfa and promises.

Call the family, call a celebration,
from Los Angeles to Ponderosa scented forest.
Gather the neighbors to witness
what marries
all of us this day,
to what humans can know of the sacred,
the presence of the True Beloved.

AND YOU WERE THERE TOO

In that undergrowth I lost myself.
Where I was wild and gentle,
with a silk petticoat, a necklace of swarming bees.

I was abuzz.
A hurricane of small white stones beating in my blood,
saying the word Paradise, over and over.

The stairway sang me upward,
over the tin steps, into the pines, blue,
the blue I painted very carefully on each child.
The note I pinned carefully on their soft sweaters.

Everything ends this way:
either poppies or wheat,
a field of red sleep,
a pasture about to be bread.

About the Author

Judyth Hill, a graduate of Sarah Lawrence College, moved to New Mexico twenty years ago where she has dedicated herself to studying and teaching creative process. She is the author of four chapbooks of poetry: *Baker's Baedaker* (Shacharit Press), *Hardwired for Love* (Pennywhistle Press), *The Goddess Cafe* (Fish Drum), and *Season With Angels* (Rockmirth Press). A larger collection of poetry, *A Presence of Angels*, was published by Sherman Asher Publishing in May 1995. To quote Ms. Hill, "I am from the Everything Matters school of writing. I have faith in the intricate connections between political, emotional, cognitive, spiritual bodies with the self and the social web; and all of this connected to our funny bone. Remember to show compassion, forgiveness and a little leg."

About the Publisher

Sherman Asher Publishing, an independent press established in 1994, is dedicated to changing the world one book at a time. We are committed to the power of truth and the craft of language expressed by publishing fine poetry, memoir, books on writing, and other books we love. You can play a role. Bring the gift of poetry into your life and the lives of others. Attend readings, teach classes, work for literacy, support your local bookstore, and buy poetry. Visit our web-site www.shermanasher.com for our latest titles, featured authors, useful links, and a calendar of author appearacnes and events.